All About

Tom Brady

Tom Brady Biography Book for Kids (With Bonus!

Coloring Pages and Videos)

All About Books

Before You Go Any Further, Get Your <u>FREE Gift</u>! (Worth $67)

Never Fear "The Call" from the School or the Hospital Again!

How to Effectively Communicate With Your Child About

Safety in a <u>Fun Way!</u>

Did you know if children are not taught properly about safety at a young age, it can potentially lead to reckless, dangerous behaviors even when they become a teenager or an adult?

Never fear "the call" from the school or the hospital with this comprehensive video course!

It'll teach you how to communicate effectively with your young ones about safety without boring them!

(Limited-Time FREE Gift)

Get It Before It Expires Here:

https://allaboutbookseries.com/freegift/

Table of Contents

Disclaimer and Note to Readers:

This book is an unofficial tribute book to Tom Brady from a fan to support his legacy.

The information in this book is provided for educational and entertainment purposes only.

The information in this book has been compiled from reliable sources. It is accurate to the best of the author's knowledge; however, the author cannot guarantee its accuracy and validity and cannot be held liable for any errors or omissions.

If you use the information contained in this book, you agree that the author is free from and not liable for any damages, costs, and expenses, including any legal fees, potentially resulting from applying any of the information provided by this guide.

The disclaimer applies to any damages or injury caused by the use and application, whether directly or indirectly, of any advice or information presented, whether for breach of contract, tort, neglect, personal injury, criminal intent, or under any other cause of action. You agree to accept all risks of using the information presented inside this book.

If an individual cites this publication as the source of information, it does not imply that the author or publisher endorse the individual or organization's knowledge. This book is an unofficial fan tribute and has not been approved or endorsed by Tom Brady or his associates.

"Tom Brady, a National Football League player" by Jeffrey Beall is licensed under Creative Commons Attribution 4.0 International license.

Introduction to Tom Brady

Tom Brady is an American football player. He is one of the greatest football players of all time. He is the quarterback of the Tampa Bay Buccaneers. He started playing football in high school. In his first two years at the University of Michigan, he was the backup quarterback.

During the draft ceremony in 2000, Brady was picked as the 199th player. The New England Patriots picked him, and he started playing as the quarterback. In this season, the Patriots won their first Super Bowl title. This made many NFL fans describe the Patriots' draft of Brady as one of the most significant NFL draft steals.

Tom Brady joined the Buccaneers in 2020 and let his greatness shine on the team. He also increased his Super Bowl victories.

As a quarterback, Tom Brady holds almost every major record, including touchdown passes, passing yards, completions, and games started, along with the most Pro Bowl selections.

In his career, Tom Brady has never had a losing season; he has the most NFL career quarterback wins, quarterback playoff wins, regular-season wins, and Super Bowl MVP awards. He is the only Super Bowl MVP for two different franchises, and the only quarterback to win a Super Bowl in three separate decades.

Tom Brady has also been praised for his long, successful career. At forty, Brady was the oldest NFL MVP and, at forty-three years, the most senior Super Bowl MVP. He is also the oldest quarterback selected to the Pro Bowl at forty-four years.

Tom Brady is the only NFL quarterback named to two all-decade teams and was named to the 100th Anniversary All-Time Team in 2019.

Tom Brady is married to a Brazilian model, Gisele Bundchen. He has three children, two sons, one from his previous relationship with American actress, Bridget Moynahan, the others, Benjamin and a daughter from his wife.

Tom Brady is worth $250 million. He has earnings accumulated from business ventures and endorsements, along with his earnings from football.

Tom Brady Documentary

http://allaboutbookseries.com/TomBradyDocumentary

Tom Brady's Early Childhood

Thomas Edward Brady, Jr. was born on August 3rd, 1977 in San Mateo, California. He is the fourth child and only son of his parents—Gailey Patricia and Thomas Brady, Sr. His father comes from an Irish background while his mother is of Swedish, German, and Norwegian descent. Tom's paternal great-great-grandparents are Irish refugees who fled to America just before the civil war. Tom's great-great uncle, Michael Buckley, Jr., was one of the first war prisoners during the second world war.

Thomas Brady, Jr. has three elder sisters: Nancy, Julie, and Maureen. The family is Catholic. Hence, Tom Brady grew up as a devout Catholic.

Growing up, Tom watched a lot of San Francisco 49ers games. One can say that influenced his love for the game. His parents would often take him to watch games; they would pile up the car and make the trip from their wealthy neighborhood in San Mateo to Candlestick Park in San Francisco. One of his fondest 49ers memories was when he was four years old. His parents had taken him to watch the 49ers game against the Dallas Cowboys. He was surprised in the first half of the game that he didn't get the #1 finger to wave at the crowd. It is funny that Tom doesn't remember much from the first half of the game except his disappointment from not getting the finger. However, in the second half of the game, the stadium was charged with so much excitement that even a three-year-old Tom could not ignore it. Everyone was cheering for Joe Montana; Tom caught on and was focused on Joe Montana. In that game, Joe Montana threw the winning touchdown to Dwight Clark.

Tom has gone on to say that Joe Montana was his idol and biggest inspiration in football.

Education

As a young boy, Tom Brady was not very athletic; he didn't have the speed that most young boys had. However, Tom liked to challenge himself, so he would challenge boys stronger than himself to race with him. They would always defeat him in the race, but rather than feel sad, he would identify his weaknesses, work on them, and then seek the boy out and rechallenge him until he defeated the boy. Then he would look for a faster boy to challenge and begin the process all over again.

He was also a gifted baseball catcher. He was naturally gifted in baseball. He has an uncanny ability to run, catch, throw, and analyze pitchers. It was second to none. People mentioned that he was meant to play baseball. However, Tom was very determined to be a footballer.

He joined the junior varsity football team at Junipero Serra High School. He was very attentive on the field. At first, Brady was not good enough to join the team. However, he joined and proved he was good enough for the team.

He became the starting quarterback in his junior year after the quarterback was injured. As a quarterback, he made new stats for the team. He also changed the team's workout routine. He added his jump rope routine.

By the end of high school, he had completed 236 of 447 passes for 3,702 yards and 31 touchdowns. Tom won the team's Most Valuable Player Award and the All-State and All-Far West honors.

Even with these awards, Tom struggled to get noticed by college scouts. He created video highlights of his best performances and sent them to different schools. However, Tom didn't have to try so hard to get noticed for baseball. He had impressed MLB scouts with his skills. The Montreal Expos drafted him in the 18th round of the 1995 MLB Draft. They saw him as a potential All-Star and one of the greatest left-handed catchers.

Then, Tom heard back from more than a dozen schools and streamlined the list to UCLA, Cal–Berkeley, USC, Illinois, and Michigan. His father hoped that he would attend Berkeley. He picked football over baseball even though he was a natural at baseball.

Assistant Coach Bill Harris recruited him for the University of Michigan in 1995. Michigan was an excellent choice for Tom Brady because he loved challenges, and Michigan was a challenge, albeit a bigger one than he imagined.

College Football Career

Tom Brady joined the Michigan Wolverines in 1995. After Assistant Coach Bill Harris drafted him, Tom found out when he was about to resume that Bill Harris was no longer the assistant coach. There was also a new head coach, Lloyd Carr. He went on to meet the new coach. Brady was redshirted all through his first season. That did not deter him. He worked hard that first year and improved a lot. He met with assistant athletic director Greg Harden weekly. Their sessions together helped Tom Brady build on his confidence and field performance.

Tom Brady played his first college game on September 26, 1996. It was a game against UCLA; Michigan was up 35-3 in the fourth quarter. His first attempt at a pass was an interception to Phillip Ward that Ward returned for a 42-yard touchdown.

Tom Brady was the backup quarterback for Brian Griese. Tom was sad because he wanted to be the starting quarterback. He was wondering how else he could convince coach Carr that he was the best guy for the job. At that point, he was considering transferring to the University of California, Berkeley. At the end of that season, he mentioned to Coach Carr that he might transfer schools. Carr asked him what his father thought and he said his father would support anything he did. Coach Carr then told him, "Tommy you've gotta worry about yourself. You've gotta go out and worry about the way you play. Not the way the guys ahead of you are playing, not the way your running back is playing, and not the way your receiver ran the route." After that conversation, Tommy promised to show Coach Carr that he was a great quarterback.

So he stayed on the team, worked harder, and saw a sports therapist for his anxiety. At this point he didn't complain about how he was treated; he just worked hard.

In 1998, the Michigan team signed a new quarterback, Drew Henson. Coach Carr had promised Drew the starting quarterback back position if he pledged to play for Michigan. Also, he announced to the press that Drew Henson was the most talented quarterback he had ever been around. Drew was All-American; he was a local hero and had broken records for his high school football team. Besides him, Tom Brady was the average QB. Tom had to compete with Drew Henson for the starting position. In some games, Tom would start, and then by the second quarter, Henson would come in.

Tom Brady, Sr. was angry about the way Tom was treated at Michigan. He mentioned that Tom was not treated kindly. Also, Coach Carr has admitted that Tom Brady faced a lot of challenges because of the situation Carr put him in.

Brady got even better; he would spend time after practice watching the football plays. He assimilated everything from the opposing players' schemes to the methods of the defense coach. And as he progressed, he could guess defenses before the ball was snapped. He knew which receivers were open. He was able to maintain his accuracy. At this point, he had become a whole different quarterback. He would often tell his teammates what happened with incomplete plays when he had not yet watched the film of the game.

During his first full year as a starter, he set new records for Michigan. He set a record for completion in a 31-16 loss to the Ohio State Buckeyes. Brady led Michigan to eight straight wins but Coach Lloyd Carr remembers the loss to Ohio State in a regular-season finale.

In the summer of 1999, Drew Henson spent his time playing for a Yankee Class A team in Tampa. When Henson returned, the coaches agreed that Brady would start, Henson would play in the second quarter, and at halftime, they would pick who would complete the game. Tom won the second-half pick in four of five games and Michigan won the five games.

In the sixth game, Carr picked Henson for the second half. Their game fell apart. Carr put in Brady, who managed a turnaround but not in time for them to win the game. At that point, the teammates wanted Brady to remain the quarterback. Coach Carr wanted to try his two-quarterback system again. So, he gave it one last try and they lost against Illinois. It was okay because Coach Carr had decided that Brady was his quarterback. Also, Tom had become friends with Henson.

As the quarterback, Brady had impressive final season numbers as a senior. His stats were 2,586 yards passing, 20 touchdowns, and six interceptions. This proved an outstanding ability to read defenses and find the open receiver. Brady would end his career by setting records and winning games, maintaining that winning attitude and extraordinary work ethic he had displayed as a young boy back in San Mateo.

The Draft

As someone who worked hard to get better and better in football, it is not unusual that Brady had aspirations to play football professionally. However, whether he was going to be a professional NFL player or not was up to scouts. In the scouting reports, Tom Brady was described as a "career backup." The funny thing about this description was that most of the coaches agreed that he was coachable and could improve on the job. The scouts also spoke about the accuracy of his passes. However, they mentioned that Brady was skinny and lacked arm strength, and did not have good footwork.

Brady was not picked until the sixth draft when New England Patriots coach Bill Belichick picked him. He was the 199th player picked and the seventh quarterback in the 2000 NFL draft.

During the draft, Tom and his family were very confident that he would be picked by the second or third round. Unfortunately, their hopes were dashed when the third turned fourth and the fourth turned to sixth.

Question to Ponder: How do you think Tom felt when his name was not picked in the early drafts?

In a 2011 interview, Tom mentioned that he was embarrassed when his name had not been picked at the beginning of the sixth round. He said that when New England mentioned they were drafting him, he was so grateful, especially because he would not have to be an insurance salesman.

Robert Kraft, the owner of the New England Patriot, recalls that Tom Brady walked up to him to introduce himself after the draft. Brady also mentioned that he was the "best decision this organization has ever made."

Tom Brady's Career

http://allaboutbookseries.com/TomBradyCareer

Professional NFL Career

Tom Brady's Rookie Season As a Professional NFL Player

After Tom Brady was drafted in 2000, he began the season as the fourth-string quarterback. He was the backup guy after starter Drew Bledsoe and his substitutes John Friesz and Michael Bishop. At the end of the season, Brady was already second on the depth chart behind starter quarterback Drew Bledsoe.

When Brady first arrived at training camp, he was excited. His teammates joked about how he was tall and skinny, but they respected him. They admired his seriousness in learning the plays.

When the season started, Tom memorized the playbook. He also lifted weights at the gym and started to build arm strength. He gained fifteen pounds of muscle and started to work on his legs. There was no time Tom Brady was not working hard to get better. He devoted his time to proving that he was more than a career backup.

That season was terrible for the Patriots; they had eleven losses. The only game Brady played was in a game against Detroit. He completed a pass for six yards.

2001 Season

In the 2001 season, the Patriots acquired veteran athletes to fortify their team. They got Bryan Cox, Otis Smith, and Roman Phifer. Unfortunately, these moves did not prevent them from losing their first few games. It was woeful.

Their next game against the Carolina Panthers was moved to the end of the season. This happened after the events of September 11, 2001. The nation was in mourning, so the NFL canceled its games for that weekend.

The Patriots played against the New York Jets. During that game, Drew Bledsoe took a hard hit and was seriously injured. He returned to play for the next series, sacrificing himself for the team. He had a sheared blood vessel and was bleeding internally. The Patriots lost that game.

In the next game, Tom Brady was the starting quarterback. The New England Patriots were playing against the Indianapolis Colts. To most people, starting Brady was an odd choice. However, Belichick was very sure that Tom was a brilliant choice.

Question to Ponder: How do you think Tom felt starting this game? If you had someone take a chance on you as Belichick did for Tom how would you feel?

In the game against the Colts, the Patriots won the game by a blowout of 44-13.

Tom Brady's First Game as a Starter

http://allaboutbookseries.com/TomBradyFirstGame

In the next game, however, the Patriots found it difficult to get past the defense of the Miami Dolphins. The Dolphins won that game. Fans of the New England Patriots started to feel like the 2001 season was going to be just as bad as the previous year. However, Lawyer Milloy, one of the players, spoke to Tom. He told Tom that he had to step up and become a more dynamic leader. According to Lawyer, Tom had done it before in Michigan and he could do it again. Tom took this advice to heart.

In the next game, they were ten points behind the San Diego Chargers late in the fourth quarter. It didn't deter the team. Tom showed that he was a capable leader. He coordinated two game-tying drives, and at the end, he set up the kicker, Adam Vinatieri, for the final field goal. The Patriots won the game by a score of 29-26.

The Patriots faced the Indiana Colts once again and defeated them. Tom threw three touchdowns in that game. He set a new record for longest play from scrimmage by letting loose a 91-yard pass to wide receiver David Patten.

In the next game, Brady played against Brian Griese. Although they played together in college, Griese was now the starting quarterback for the Denver Broncos. Once again, Tom Brady and the Patriots found it challenging to counter the defense of the Denver Broncos. The Patriots lost this game. Tom didn't dwell on the loss. He took it as an opportunity to learn. He watched the recording of the game, learned from his mistakes, and moved on to win two games back to back by defeating the Atlanta Falcons and the Buffalo Bills.

In the next game, the Patriots were to play against the St. Louis Rams at home. Sports enthusiasts predicted that this was going to be a walk in the park for The Rams. Tom Brady started to prove them wrong from the first quarter. He played like a seasoned player. Unfortunately, in the second quarter, running back Antowain Smith delivered a costly fumble. The Rams capitalized on this fumble. The Patriots lost this game. However, Brady had proved himself to the team and fans. He had convinced them that he could lead the team to victory.

Then Bledsoe recovered. He was cleared to play. Many people thought there would be a quarterback rivalry between Bledsoe and Brady. However, Coach Belichick put Tom as the starting quarterback for the rest of the season. Drew Bledsoe was angry about the decision, but he came around stating that he would do his best to make sure that the team won. While Drew

24

Bledsoe was injured, he helped Tom with his rehabilitation. Also, Bledsoe felt that he lost his job as a starter not because Tom was a better player but because he (Drew) got injured. This caused a strain in their relationship because Tom held Drew Bledsoe in high regard.

Question to Ponder: Have you ever had issues with a teammate you used to get along with? How did you get over it?

The next game was against the New Orleans Saint. Once again the Patriots won with a blowout, 34-17. This game against the Saints assured the New England team and fans that Belichick had made a great decision by starting Tom Brady. They also won 17-16 against the Jets. The Patriots were leading 6-5, and fans were believing in the team again.

Tom didn't let the issues with Bledsoe deter him on the field. He still went on to do great things on the field. They defeated the Cleveland Browns and gave the Buffalo Bills a loss in overtime. The win against the Bills set the Patriots against the Miami Dolphins for a game that would give the winner a home-field advantage and a first-round bye in the upcoming playoffs. The Patriots defeated the Dolphins 20-13.

In the next game, the Patriots played against the Carolina Panthers and soundly defeated them 38-6. At this point, Brady hoped to be in the Super Bowl.

After that game, Tom Brady learned that he, alongside Lawyer Milloy, had been chosen to play in the Pro Bowl.

Question to Ponder: What would be your reaction if you were ever chosen to play in the pro bowl?

Tom was ecstatic; his hard work was paying off. He had a newfound fan base who believed in him.

Also, his wish to be in the Super Bowl was looking feasible. The Patriots defeated the Pittsburgh Steelers, and they were crowned the American Football Conference (AFC) champions. They were to go against the St. Louis Rams at the Super Bowl. They played the game at the Louisiana Superdome in New Orleans. This was the Ram's third Super Bowl appearance.

The Rams played well, outgaining the New England Patriots 427–267 in total yards. The Patriots trailed by 17-3 by the first quarter. The Rams got scored a touchdown. Kurt Warner of the St Louis Rams, threw another touchdown pass, tying the game to 17-17 in the fourth quarter. Luckily for the Patriots, with 1:30 minutes to end the game, Brady led his team to set up Adam Vinatieri, the kicker, to score a 48-yard field goal just as the time was up. The Patriots won the game 20-17. Tom Brady was the MVP of the game.

http://allaboutbookseries.com/TomBradyFirstSuperBowl

Question to Ponder: How do you think Tom Brady felt about winning the Super Bowl and MVP of the game?

"Tom Brady - New England Patriots" by Mike Lizzi is licensed under CC BY 2.0.

2002 Season

The new season came with Tom Brady unprepared. He was a Pro Bowl player, and the fame that came with it was a lot. It was almost too much to handle. Before winning the Super Bowl, Brady had time to watch game clips, hit the weight room, and work on his passing. The off-season was hectic for him. It was filled with invitations to parties, interviews, and talk shows. Everyone wanted to talk to Pro Bowl player Brady.

The New England Patriots also brought reinforcement to the new season. They acquired two tight ends, Christian Fauria and Cameron Cleveland. They also added a very fast wide receiver, Deion Branch. People could not stop talking about how they were excited to see what the Patriots would do with the new additions to the team.

The Patriots started the season well. It seemed that they didn't miss anything from the previous season. Their first three games even looked as if they had gotten better. Tom Brady was starting to feel confident. Unfortunately, the four games that followed were not so good. In fact, the Patriots lost all four. This had Brady questioning himself as a passer.

Question to Ponder: How do you think Tom Brady felt when he went from winning games to losing at a stretch?

Nevertheless, it was not all Tom's fault. The opposing team had found a weakness in the Patriot's plays and had capitalized on it. The Patriots had no running game; the defenders had to cover receivers. Brady had no open receiver to throw to; this was very evident in their four back-to-back losses. This caused the team to struggle that season. The Patriots were playing catch-up in games. Brady's arm was getting tired; it was even affecting his accuracy on the field. Our superstar became the target of backlash and questions. He didn't make excuses; rather he worked harder.

With very slim chances of making the playoffs, the Patriots were facing the Dolphins once again. They had a come-from-behind win, defeating the Dolphins 27-24. At this point, what they needed to make the playoffs was for the Browns and New York Jets to lose their games. Unfortunately for the Patriots, both teams won, causing the Patriots to miss the playoffs.

Although the team didn't make the playoffs, Brady had good stats for that year. He threw for 3,763 yards, scored 28 touchdowns, and had a completion rating of over 60 percent. Brady didn't care about the stats; the only number he cared about was the win-loss number, and he wasn't happy with the ending record. He wanted to make a repeat trip to the Super Bowl, but 2002 was not the year. For the Patriots, this was the last year that they didn't win at least ten games in the regular season until 2020. For Brady, this was the only season where he started half the games in the regular season, and his team didn't make the playoffs.

2003 Season

One thing that Brady learned from the 2002 season was to be disciplined in his preparations for the football season.

The 2003 season was challenging, but Brady was determined to succeed in the new season. In the last game in the previous season, Tom's shoulder was separated. Many people told him to fix it with surgery, but Tom declined. He was going to work on the shoulder. The team didn't disclose this injury to the public. They didn't want fans and commentators to have something to question in the new season.

The new season started for the New England Patriots with a game against the Buffalo Bills. Unfortunately, it was a blowout for the Patriots. They lost the game 31-0. It was brutal. Brady was repeatedly criticized; Coach Belichick was not spared from the criticism. Rumors spread that the team lost faith in Brady and the coach. For any sports team, this was a challenging position to be thrust into; having the team distrust the most important members of the team is not a good thing. Fans were wondering how the Patriots were going to come back from this.

Regardless of what had happened in the game against the Bills, Tom vowed that he was not going to have a repeat of the 2002 season. The next game was against the Philadelphia Eagles. When the Patriots came on the field, it was evident that there was a shift. Miraculously, they played better than the last game, defeating the Eagles, 31-10. It appeared like they were back in the Super Bowl form. In their next game against the Jets, they won 23-16. Then they lost the next game to the Washington Redskins. It didn't stop them, though.

The team was struggling; players were getting injured here and there. Brady's shoulder was acting up. He didn't let it show on the field. The Patriots kept winning; they had fifteen back-to-back wins. They even had a revenge match with the Bills where they defeated them 31-0.

At this point, they were looking at the playoffs. The criticism of Tom Brady had been silenced with the wins.

During the playoffs, the Patriots defeated the Tennessee Titans (17-14) and then defeated the Indianapolis Colts in the AFC Championship. The Patriots were going to the Super Bowl once again, and they would be facing the Carolina Panthers.

The game was what you expect from two solid opponents. The Patriots had a strong defense. They led the game with the Panthers not far behind. The Panthers tied the game in the fourth quarter. At this point, it looked like the game was going into overtime. Brady was not worried. With the calm and experience of a seasoned veteran, he led the team within the field goal range. Adam Vinatieri took the field and split the uprights, sending the Patriots back to the podium with a final score of 32–29 over the Panthers.

Now Brady was a two-time Super Bowl winner. This time he had learned from his previous off-season mistakes and was determined not to repeat them. He attended the events that he was invited to, but he still incorporated his off-season workouts.

2004 Season

The 2004 season started well for the Patriots. They worked on their running game and added superstar Corey Dillon to the team. They were dominating their games. They won games against the Colts (27–24), the Cardinals (23–12), the Bills (31–17), the Dolphins (24–10), the Seahawks (30–20), and the Jets (13–7).

The Patriots were having the time of their lives. Then, Corey Dillon got injured. This could not have happened at a more tragic time. The Patriots were to play against the Pittsburgh Steelers at their next game. The Steelers capitalized on Corey's injury and then gave the Patriots their first loss of the season with a score of 34-20. This also ended their winning streak of 21 games that had carried over from the previous season. After that game, Corey rejoined the lineup, and the Patriots won six back-to-back games. Unfortunately, this streak was interrupted when Tom Brady threw an interception in the game against the Miami Dolphins, causing them to lose with a final score of 29-28. It did not matter; the Patriots finished that season with a record of 14 wins to 2 losses. They were standing at the top of the AFC divisional Championship table.

Brady's game had also seen a lot of improvement that season. His numbers were stunning. He had 3,692 yards and 28 touchdowns. The most significant improvement was his throwing of the deep ball. Right from his NFL draft, coaches had mentioned that he was unable to throw deep. However, in the 2004 season, he had pulled off 52 passes of 20 yards and ten passes of more than 40 yards, proving once again that his weakness did not limit him, and he was willing to work on his weakness.

In the playoffs, the Patriots had their first game with the Indianapolis Colts. The Colts were a worthy opponent and a lot of football fans felt that the Colts were going to send the Patriots home. Fortunately for the Patriots, they won the game 20-3.

The next game was against the Steelers. The Patriots won that game with their solid defense. Once again they were off to the Super Bowl. The Patriots were playing against the Philadelphia Eagles. The Patriots played well and defeated the Eagles with a final score of 24-21. Tom Brady won another Super Bowl.

2005 Season

When the Patriots went to the 2005 season, they were not as strong as they had been. The team had lost some of its strong players. For instance, they lost two of their coordinators, Charlie Weiss and Romeo Crenel. They also lost Tedy Bruschi, their star linebacker, to a stroke. Ted Johnson retired and Ty Law had to go due to salary cap reasons.

The Patriots started the season with a win against the Oakland Raiders, with a final score of 30-20. Then they suffered a loss to the Carolina Panthers. They won their next game against the Pittsburgh Steelers. They lost their next game to the San Diego Chargers. The team had a tumult. Losses followed their wins. It was exhausting.

The Patriots made it to the playoffs; they won their first game against the Jacksonville Jaguars. Unfortunately, they lost their next game to the Denver Broncos. So, the Patriots didn't make it to the Super Bowl.

2006 Season

The Patriots started a new season without their previous wide receivers. Deion Branch waited for a new contract but was traded. David Givens became a free agent and left the team. They recruited Jabar Gaffney, a free agent, and Reche Caldwell.

The team won its first game of the season against the Buffalo Bills. The second game also went well. However, in their next game against the Denver Broncos, the team had their first season loss. In the next game, the team brought their A-game and defeated the Cincinnati Bengals. They went further to win three more games before losing to the Indianapolis Colts 27-20. They also lost their next game to the New York Jets 17-14. They had two consecutive losses, which was not a good look for the team. For the first time in years, they had a losing streak. Tom Brady's plays were also criticized. He was sacked four times and threw an interception late in the fourth quarter.

In the next game, the Patriots were back. The game was against the Green Bay Packers, and the Patriots won with a blowout 35-0. They won their next two games before suffering a blowout against the Miami Dolphins, 21-0. They now had four losses, and their record was 9-4. They won their next three games, which sent them to the playoffs.

They won the wildcard game against the Jets and the divisional round against the San Diego Chargers. At the AFC Championship Game, the Patriots went against the Indianapolis

Colts; the Colts won the game even though the Patriots led the game with 21-3 at the beginning. The Colts went on to win the Super Bowl that year.

2007 Season

The 2007 season started with a scandal for the Patriots. Coach Belichick, along with the Patriots organization, was punished for recording the Jets' defensive situation from an unauthorized location in the old Meadowlands Stadium. As punishment, The NFL deprived the Patriots of a first draft pick. They also fined the team along with head coach Bill Belichick. However, days later, the NFL closed the case and destroyed evidence.

Question to Ponder: How do you think Tom Brady and his team members felt when they were involved with the spy gate cheating scandal?

This was a challenging period for the Patriots. They were under surveillance for their first few games. They lost support from members of the public. People now referred to them as "Cheatriots."

However, the Patriots didn't let the accusations define them. They ensured that they proved to the public that they didn't have to cheat to win. Sports fans believed that the Patriots were stomping their opponents just for entertaining the idea that they were cheating. Some of the players later confirmed this to ESPN's Seth Wickersham in 2013. They said, "It was a matter of, we're not just going to stick it to you, we're going to stick it to you a little more than we usually have." That year they worked harder than normal.

In their first game, while under surveillance from the NFL, they still defeated the New York Jets 38-14. The victory didn't stop there. They had back-to-back wins and made it to the Super Bowl. Unfortunately, they lost the Super Bowl game to the New York Giants 17-14.

Even with the Super Bowl loss, football enthusiasts and critics have mentioned that the 2007 season was a turning point in Brady's career. They have compared it with Dan Marino's 1984 season, Joe Montana's 1989 season, Steve Young's 1994 season, Kurt Warner's 1999 season, and even Peyton Manning's 2004 season.

The Patriots scored 331 points in their first eight games. They scored 314 points on the road. The Patriots had 41 more touchdowns than their competitors. In their 16-0 season, in ten of their victories, they had 21 or more points.

It was one of the greatest offense plays the NFL had seen.

It seemed that Brady aged like wine when it came to football. At age thirty, his plays were better than in previous seasons. He led the NFL in completion percentage with 68.9, 4,806 passing yards, 50 touchdown passes, and 8.3 yards per attempt. He achieved all these, throwing only eight interceptions and was sacked 21 times. It was beautiful to watch.

While most of his records that season have been surpassed, there are just some quarterback seasons that are always worth mentioning, and the 2007 season is one of them.

2008 Season

Compared to the 2007 season, the 2008 season for the Patriots was average. The Patriots went from having a record of 16-0 in the season to 11-5. The season began with the opening game against the Kansas City Chiefs. The Patriots won the game. Unfortunately, Tom Brady was injured. During the game, he was hit on his knee by Benard Pollard. The hit resulted in a torn ACL and MCL. Pollard was not penalized for the injury. Tom was escorted off the field by athletic trainers.

Question to Ponder: How do you think Tom Brady felt when he was injured and found out he could not play for the rest of the season?

For the rest of the season, Matt Cassel replaced Tom Brady. He led the team to a win in their next game against the New York Jets, but they tanked 38-13 in the game against the Miami Dolphins. This loss ended their 21-game winning streak. The team made it to the last week of the regular season with an 11-5 record but needed either the Baltimore Ravens or Miami Dolphins to lose a game so they could make it to the playoffs. Unfortunately, both teams won. They also had the same 11-5 record as the Patriots. Unfortunately for the Patriots, the Dolphins won the AFC East division, qualifying them for the playoffs. The Ravens qualified for the playoffs as a wildcard team. So for the first time since 2002, the Patriots did not make it to the playoffs. This made the Patriots the first team with eleven wins not to make the playoffs after the football season expanded to a 12-team playoff in 1990. They were also the first team that didn't make it to the playoffs after going undefeated in their previous season.

Tom Brady is Injured by Benard Pollard

http://allaboutbookseries.com/TomBrady2008Injury

2009 Season

After the 2008 season, the Patriots went through changes. The changes were mainly within the coaching and personnel staff. Scott Pioli, the Vice President of Player Personnel left the club to become the General Manager of the Kansas City Chiefs. Josh McDaniel, the team's offensive coordinator, became the head coach of the Denver Broncos. There were also changes among the team. Matt Cassel, Richard Seymour, and Mike Vrabel were traded. Tedy Bruschi and Rodney Harrison also retired from the league.

The season began with the Patriots' 50th anniversary game against the Buffalo Bills. They won the game. They suffered their first loss in their next game against the New York Jets (16-9).

They won the next two games but lost the next game to the Denver Broncos. The season was filled with a rollercoaster of wins and losses. They finished the season with a 10-6 record. They got into the wildcard game for the playoffs. They played against the Baltimore Ravens and lost the game.

2010 Season

For the new season, the Patriots had no offensive or defensive coordinator. They traded wide receiver, Randy Moss. Deion Branch also returned to the team. The season began for the Patriots in an opening game against the Cincinnati Bengals. They won the game. The next game, they had their first loss of the season in the game against the Jets. They had back-to-back wins until the ninth week when they lost to the Cleveland Browns. The Patriots had back-to-back wins until the end of the regular season, finishing with a record of 14-2. They made it to the divisional round of the playoffs. At halftime, the Patriots were behind 14-3. They tried to but could not recover from the halftime deficit. They lost the game to the New York Jets 28-31.

The season was good for Tom Brady. He beat his previous 2007 NFL TD to INT ratio record with 9:1. He made 335 consecutive pass attempts without an interception. He was also awarded the NFL MVP. Tom Brady had a passer rating of 110.0 with 3900 yards. He made 36 touchdowns with four interceptions.

Football statistics also mentioned that the 2010 Patriots' Offense was the best-calculated offense in their history.

2011 Season

This Patriots season was dedicated to Myra Kraft, the wife of Robert Kraft, the owner of the New England Patriots football team. She died earlier in 2011, and the players chose to honor her by wearing her initials "MHK" on their jerseys. The team won their first two games but lost their third game to Buffalo Bills (34-31). They won the next three games but lost the game with the Steelers. The Steelers played well in that game. They kept Brady contained while pacing the Patriot's wide receiver Wes Welker. Tom Brady passed for two touchdowns and threw a total of only 198 yards. Unfortunately for the Patriots, their attempts at a comeback were thwarted. The Patriots missed a field goal in the third quarter, punted four times, and could not recover a field goal within two minutes of the end of the game. It was not a good game for the Patriots, mainly because they were defeated in their house.

In the next game, the Patriots lost again to the New York Giants (24-20). They won the next eight games, finishing the regular season with a 13-3 record. They made it to the playoffs. They defeated the Denver Broncos and Baltimore Ravens, winning the AFC Championship and making it to the Super Bowl.

At the Super Bowl, the Patriots were playing against the New York Giants. This was Tom Brady's seventh Super Bowl trip. The Patriots were not their best at this game. They had four costly drops in the fourth quarter that affected the game's results. Wes Welker dropped a wide-open pass; Deion Branch consecutively dropped two passes; then Aaron Hernandez dropped the final one. Rob Gronkowski had a high ankle sprain. Tom Brady passed the ball to an injured Gronkowski while trying to avoid sacks; this, in turn, led to an interception. Then he threw the ball from an end zone to nobody in particular; it resulted in a safety. The New England defense had an inferior tackling game. In the end, they lost the game, 21-17.

The Super Bowl game might not have been Brady's best, but he got a couple of awards that season. In the first week of the season, he won AFC Offensive Player of the Week and FedEx Express NFL Player of the Week. He still won the AFC Offensive Player of the Week in the second week and 16th week.   He was the AFC Offensive Player of the Month for November, December/January.

2012 Season

The 2012 season came with some changes in the team. The Patriots signed Brandon Lloyd to replace Chad Ochocinco, who had struggled on the team. The Patriots also signed Joseph Addai. The 2012 season was the team's 43rd in the NFL. In true Patriots' fashion, the Patriots won their first game of the regular season. The team lost the next game against The Arizona Cardinals. This was the first time the Patriots had lost a game to the Cardinals since 1991. They lost the next game to the Baltimore Ravens 31-30. They won the next two games but lost in the sixth week to the Seattle Seahawks. They went on to win the next seven games and then lost to the San Francisco 49ers 41-34. They went on to finish the season by defeating the Miami Dolphins with a blowout score of 28-0. They qualified for the playoffs winning the divisional game against the Houston Texans. They, however, lost the AFC championship to the Baltimore Ravens. They finished the season with a record of 13-5. For the Patriots, this was far from a good season. Tom Brady made a lot of bad plays this season. Compared to the rest of his career, he could have had a better season. His stats were good. He threw 34 touchdowns, eight interceptions, and 4,827 yards.

2013 Season

The 2013 season seemed promising for the Patriots. They started the season with consecutive wins from their first four games but lost their fifth game of the season to the Cincinnati Bengals. They won the next game against the New Orleans Saints but lost their seventh game to the Jets. They won the next two games but lost in the 11th week to the Carolina Panthers. They won the next four games and then lost to the Miami Dolphins. They went on to finish the season with a 12-4 record. They won the divisional championship, defeating the Indianapolis Colts. The Patriots' ride to the Super Bowl ended in the next game when they were defeated by the Denver Broncos. They didn't win the AFC Championship. This was not a good game for Tom Brady. He was 29-54 for 320 yards, one touchdown, and two interceptions that came late in the fourth quarter. They lost by fifteen points.

Question to Ponder: How do you think Tom Brady felt after the loss?

Tom's stats were 4,343 total yards, 25 touchdowns, and 11 interceptions.

2014 Season

In the last season, the Patriots were one game away from the Super Bowl. For the team, it had been ten years since their last Super Bowl win. They had qualified for the playoffs nine times since then. They had, however, appeared in two Super Bowl games since then.

The team started the new season with a loss to the Miami Dolphins. This didn't bother the Patriots. Brady led the team to a blowout victory against the Miami Vikings. Their next loss was in the game with the Kansas City Chiefs. It was a blowout, 41-14. Fans and critics had a lot to say. They said that Tom Brady was playing the worst football of his career. A lot of people mentioned that this was the end of the Patriots football. However, the Patriots didn't let that loss define them. They came back and won the next seven games. Their winning streak ended in their game against the Green Bay Packers. They won the next three games, finishing the regular season with a loss to the Buffalo Bills. They finished the season with a 12-4 record. They went on to the playoffs and won the AFC championship. Before the championship game, the general manager of the Indianapolis Colts sent an email to the NFL, complaining about the air pressure of the football used by the New England team. During the championship game, the league officials decided to test the balls used by the New England team. The balls used by the Patriots were less than the legal requirement. The balls were re-inflated, and the Patriots still won the championship game. However, this led to a lengthy investigation of Brady. Tom denied knowing anything about the deflated footballs. Paul Weiss and his team of investigators mentioned that with their evidence, they could prove that Tom Brady was aware of the deflated footballs. Tom still denied any knowledge of the deflated football.

Question to Ponder: How do you think Tom felt about the scandal and investigation and the threat it posed to his career?

The Patriots made it to the Super Bowl. They defeated the Seattle Seahawks and won the Super Bowl. Brady played well that season. He threw 33 touchdowns, 4109 yards, and nine interceptions.

The investigation about the deflated balls continued. The league stated that as punishment, Brady would be suspended for the first four games of the next season. The Patriots would also have to pay a fine of $1 million.

Question to Ponder: How do you think Brady felt about the punishment?

Tom Brady was quiet about the situation. However, his agent kept defending him and calling out the credibility of Paul Weiss.

Brady tried to appeal the four-game suspension, but commissioner Goodell upheld the suspension stating that Brady was generally aware of the illegal deflation of the ball.

In August 2015, Judge Berman of the Second Circuit Court of Appeals nullified the suspension. Commissioner Goodell mentioned that the league was appealing the judgment. However, it was stated that while they demand an appeal, the NFL could not suspend Brady from playing.

2015 Season

The new season started well for the Patriots. Brady was not suspended; it felt good to play with the team. They started the season by winning ten games in a row. With a record of 10-0 in this new season, the Patriots were riding high from their Super Bowl win. Then they got to the twelfth week, and the losses began. They first lost to the Denver Broncos. The following week, they lost to the Philadelphia Eagles. They won the next two games and lost the final two games of the regular season, finishing the season with a 12-4 record. They got to the playoffs but lost the AFC Championship to the Denver Broncos 20-18.

Brady's stats were impressive compared to the previous season. He threw 36 touchdowns, 4,770 yards, and seven interceptions. He had a rating of 102.2.

Later in April, there was an appeal in the case of the illegally deflated footballs. A three-judge panel of the Second Circuit Court of Appeals heard the case. The major decision was, "We hold that the commissioner properly exercised his broad discretion under the collective bargaining agreement and that his procedural rulings were properly grounded in that agreement and did not deprive Brady of fundamental fairness. Accordingly, we reverse the district court's judgment and remand with instructions to confirm the award." The ruling was more about affirming Goodell's authority than the deflated balls.

Brady's team asked for a second hearing, but they were denied by the second circuit court of appeals. They were told to go to the Supreme Court if they wanted to appeal.

Later in July 2016, Tom Brady announced that he would not continue with the legal process but accept the suspension and the dock in his play.

Question to Ponder: Why do you think Tom Brady decided to stop the legal process?

2016 Season

The 2016 season began after the whole "deflategate" scandal. Tom Brady was suspended for four games and during that time, he was not allowed anywhere near the Patriots' facility. He was also not allowed to have contact with his team members. For the first four games, the Patriots had a record of 3-1 led by backup quarterbacks Jacoby Brissett and Jimmy Garoppolo.

Tom Brady returned to play in the game against the Browns. Brady came prepared for his first game post-suspension. He was on fire. In the first half, he passed for 276 yards and two short touchdowns. He helped Bennet to make a 37-yarder in the third quarter. At the end of the game, He passed for 406 yards and made three touchdowns leading to a 33-13 victory over the Browns.

They won the next three games but lost in the tenth week to the Seattle Seahawks. They went on to win the rest of their games, finishing the regular season with a 14-2 record. This was better than the previous seasons. They won the divisional games and went on to win the AFC Championship. Once again, the team was going to the Super Bowl. The team played against the Atlanta Falcons, who were seeking their first Super Bowl win. The match started well for the Falcons. By halftime, the Falcons were leading by 21-3. This became a 28-3 lead halfway through the third quarter. In the final minutes of the game, the Patriots scored points that led to a tie in the game. The game went to overtime, and the Patriots received the kickoff. They scored a touchdown and won the game 34-28. This was the biggest comeback in Super Bowl history. The King of Comeback victories was back. The Patriots broke the record for more than thirty teams. Tom Brady broke his record of 43 completed passes, 62 pass attempts, and 466 passing yards. He also won the MVP of the game, making him the oldest to receive the award at age 39. It was his fourth time winning that award.

2017 Season

The Patriots came into the new season still high from winning Super Bowl LI. Their first game was against the Kansas City Chiefs. Tom Brady started the game with a nine-play, 73-yard touchdown. Things were looking great for the Patriots when the Chiefs fumbled on their first offensive series. However, the Chiefs came back with a vendetta to win. The Patriots lost the game 42-27. They won the next two games, then lost in the fourth week to the Carolina Panthers. They consecutively won the next eight games and were on their way to maintaining the same record as the previous season until they lost to the Miami Dolphins. The team won the rest of their games and made it to the playoffs. They won the AFC Championship and made it to the Super Bowl. The championship win made Tom Brady the oldest quarterback to win the AFC Championship.

They were going to defend their previous Super Bowl championship against the Philadelphia Eagles. At this point, the Patriots were the only team to appear in the Super Bowl ten times. The Patriots had the opportunity to tie with the Pittsburgh Steelers as the team with the most Super Bowl wins. Unfortunately for the Patriots, they didn't win the Super Bowl that year. The Eagles converted a fumble into a field goal. With a few minutes to the end of the game, Tom Brady tried a Hail Mary pass that fell incomplete. The loss made the Patriots the fifth defending champion to lose the following year's game. They also had the most Super Bowl losses with five games.

Tom Brady passed for 4577 yards; he made 32 touchdowns and eight interceptions that season.

2018 Season

The new season started with the Patriots' game against the Houston Texans. The Patriots won the game but went on to have two double-digit losses in weeks two and three. They won the next games until week ten when they lost to the Titans. The remaining weeks were a rollercoaster of wins and losses. They finished the season with a record of 11-5. They got into the playoffs, winning the Divisional Championship and the AFC Championship. They went on to play in the Super Bowl against the St Louis Rams. This was a rematch of Super Bowl XXXVI, where the Patriots won 20-17. In this game, the Patriots also won 13-3. This tied them with the Steelers as the team with the most Super Bowl wins.

Tom Brady passed for 4,355 yards; he had 29 touchdowns and 11 interceptions.

2019 Season

Before the beginning of the 2019 season, Tom Brady mentioned that he might retire. However, later in August 2019, he signed a two-year extension with the Patriots worth $70 million. However, the deal expired in 2019, stating that in 2020, Tom Brady was a free agent.

Riding on their Super Bowl win in the previous season, the Patriots came with the energy to win another Super Bowl. They started the regular season with an 8-0 record. In the ninth week, they lost their first season to the Baltimore Ravens. Brady mentioned that he was very frustrated with the Patriots' team. He mentioned that he was the only 8-0 unhappy quarterback. The season continued with a roller coaster of wins and losses. The Patriots finished the season with a 12-4 record. They qualified for the wild card game but lost to the Tennessee Titans. This was the end of their journey in the 2019 season.

At this point, there were speculations that Brady might not return for the next season. Tom and Belichick discussed his return the following season, but they never reached a decision.

In March 2020, Brady announced through his Instagram that he was leaving the New England Patriots after 20 seasons. He signed with the Tampa Bay Buccaneers three days later.

2020 Season

The 2020 season for Brady was a new beginning. He would be playing for a new team: the Tampa Bay Buccaneers. At the end of his last season with the Patriots, Brady suffered a torn MCL in his left knee. He had to have surgery to fix it. He played the whole season with a torn MCL. While the Tampa Bay team was not an all-star team, Brady played with them and changed their 7-9 regular season record to an 11-5 record. It was a huge win. They qualified for the wild card round and defeated the Washington Football Team to be eligible for the divisional championship. They won the NFC Championship and advanced to the Super Bowl. Tom Brady had his twelfth Super Bowl appearance and won the seventh Super Bowl of his career.

Tom Brady's Seventh Super Bowl Win

http://allaboutbookseries.com/TomBrady7thSuperBowl

In the regular season, Tom Brady passed for 4,633 yards; he made 40 touchdowns against 12 interceptions.

2021 Season

Tom Brady and the Tampa Bay Buccaneers began the 2021 season still high from the previous Super Bowl win. They finished the season with a 13-4 record and played in the wild-card game. They won the game but lost the divisional championship to the Los Angeles Rams. This loss ended their run in the playoffs.

This was a good season for Tom Brady. He made his 600th touchdown pass of his NFL career. Although the team win in the playoffs, Brady's season was filled with highlights.

Tom Brady Jr: Best Highlights

http://allaboutbookseries.com/TomBradySeasonHighlights

Tom Brady announced that he was retiring in early 2022. Forty days later he announced that he was coming out of retirement.

Tom Brady's Awards, Honors, and Lifetime Achievements

As a football player, Thomas Brady has made quite a lot of achievements awarding him many honors. He has currently won the Super Bowl Championship seven times; six of which were won with the New England Patriots and one with Tampa Bay Buccaneers. This is quite an achievement because it is the most titles for any individual player. Not only that, but he also has quite a notable NFL record, which is listed below. He is well-renowned in the football community for achieving many unbreakable records in the course of his career.

His NFL records for both the regular season and playoffs:

- He has the most NFL Championships by a player (7)

- He has the most championships in professional football history by a quarterback (7)

- He has the most games won by a player (278)

- He has the most games played by a quarterback (365)

- He has the most games started by a quarterback (363)

- He has the most games played by a skill position player (365)

- He has the most games started by a skill position player (363)

- He has the most combined passing attempts (13,172)

- He has the most combined pass completions (8,428)

- He has the most combined touchdown passes (710)

- He has the most combined passing yards (97,569)

- He has the most game-winning drives (67)

- He has the most fourth-quarter comebacks (51)

- He has the most times sacked (622)

- He has the most players throwing a touchdown pass to (92)

Tom Brady's NFL Records for Regular Seasons:

- He has the most games won by a player (243)

- He has the most games played by a non-kicker (318)

- He has the most games started by a skill position player (316)

- He is the fourth NFL player to beat all 32 teams

- He has the most seasons with 40+ touchdown passes: 3 (tied)

- He is one of two quarterbacks to have multiple 5000-yard seasons

- He has the most games with 2+ touchdown passes (198)

- He has the best touchdown to interception ratio in a season (28:2)

- He has the most wins on the road by a quarterback (110)

- He has the most wins at home by a quarterback (133)

- He has the most wins in one regular season by a quarterback (16)

- He is the only quarterback to have three consecutive games with over 300 passing yards, over 3 touchdown passes and 0 interceptions.

- He has the most seasons with 35+ touchdown passes (6 of which were tied with Aaron Rodgers)

- He has the most regular-season starts by a player (316)

- He is the oldest quarterback to lead the league in passing yards: 44 (5,316 yards: 2021)

- He has the most yards in a single season for a quarterback aged 40 and older: age 44 (5,316)

- He is the oldest player to win NFL MVP (Won it at age 40)

- He is the oldest position player to be named first-team All-Pro (Named at age 40)

- He has the most career passing yards with one team (New England Patriots): 74,571

- He has the most career passing yards (84,520)

- He has the most career passing touchdowns with one team: 541

- He has the most Pro Bowl selections (15)

- He has the most seasons quarterbacking for one team (20)

- He has the most career pass completions (7,263)

- He has the most career passing attempts (11,317)

- He has the most career touchdown passes (624)

- He has the most seasons as passing touchdowns leader (5)

- He has the most consecutive 10-win seasons as the starting quarterback (13)

- He has the most consecutive 11-win seasons as starting quarterback: (12)

- He has the most consecutive seasons on team 9–7 or better: 21

- He has the most touchdown passes in a season as starting quarterback aged 40 or older: 43 (2021)

- He is the only quarterback to have 40 passing touchdowns in a season in both the AFC (50; 2007) and the NFC (40; 2020)

Tom Brady's NFL Records for Playoffs:

- He has the most consecutive seasons in the NFL playoffs by a team, player, or head coach: 13

- He has the most wins (35)

- He has the most games started (47)

- He has the most starting quarterbacks beaten (QB): 27

- He has the most teams beaten (QB): 19

- He has won in the most stadiums (QB): 13

- He has the most games won by a starting quarterback: 35

- He has the most consecutive wins by a starting quarterback: 10 (2001–2005)

- He has the most postseason touchdown passes to different players: 34

- He has the most postseason road wins by a quarterback: 7 (He is tied with Joe Flacco)

- He is the oldest player to throw a touchdown pass (44 years of age)

- He has the most consecutive wins to start a career by a starting quarterback: 10 (2001, 2003–2005)

- He has the most career home wins by a starting quarterback (21)

- He has the most consecutive home wins by a starting quarterback: 9 (2013–2019)

- He has the most touchdown passes: 86

- He has the most touchdown passes between a quarterback and receiver: 14 (with Rob Gronkowski)

- He has the most passing yards with a total of 13,049

- He has the most passing yards in a single playoff game: 505 (Super Bowl LII)

- He has the most passes completed (1,165)

- He has the most passes attempted (1,855)

- He has the most passes intercepted (39)

- He has the most division titles won by a starting quarterback (18)

- He has the most appearances in the NFL conference championship by a starting quarterback (14)

- He has the most NFL conference championship wins by a starting quarterback (10)

- He is the oldest quarterback to win an AFC title game aging 41 years, 5 months, 17 days

- He is also the oldest quarterback to win an NFC title game aging 43 years, 5 months, 21 days

- He has the most career 300+ passing yard games: 18

- He has the most game-winning drives: 14

- He has the most fourth-quarter comebacks (9)

- He has the most multi-TD pass games with a total of 28

Tom's Superbowl Records:

- He has the most wins as a player: 7

- He has the most wins as the starting QB: 7

- He has more wins than anyone in the NFL franchise has in total

- He is the only quarterback to win the Super Bowl for both the AFC and NFC

- He has the most Super Bowl MVPs: 5

- He is one of only two quarterbacks to win a Super Bowl for two separate teams (the other being Peyton Manning)

- He has the most touchdown passes: 21

- He has the most passing yards: 3,039

- He has the most passes completed: 277

- He has the most passes attempted: 421

- He has the most passes completed in the first half of a single Super Bowl: 20 (XLIX)

- He has the most passes completed in a single Super Bowl: 43 (LI)

- He has the most passes attempted in a single Super Bowl: 62 (LI)

- He has the most passing yards in a single Super Bowl: 505 (LII)

- Tom has the most appearance in Super Bowl (10)

- He has the most passing attempts without an interception in a single Super Bowl game: 48 (XLII & LII)

- He is the oldest QB to start a Super Bowl: 43 years, 6 months, and 5 days

- He is the oldest QB to win a Super Bowl: 43 years, 6 months, and 5 days

- He is the oldest player to win Super Bowl MVP: 43 years, 6 months, and 5 days

- He is the oldest QB from the AFC to start a Super Bowl: 41 years, 6 months, and 0 days

- He is the oldest QB from the AFC to win a Super Bowl: 41 years, 6 months, and 0 days

- He is the oldest player from the AFC to win Super Bowl MVP: 39 years, 6 months, and 2 days

- He is also the oldest QB from the NFC to start a Super Bowl: 43 years, 6 months, and 5 days

- He is the oldest QB from the NFC to win a Super Bowl: 43 years, 6 months, and 5 days

- He is the oldest player from the NFC to win Super Bowl MVP: 43 years, 6 months, and 5 days

- He has the most consecutive completions in a single Super Bowl: 16 (XLVI)

- He also has the most game-winning drives: 6

Thomas Brady's Awards and Honors

Thomas won a Sports Emmy Award for the category of

- Outstanding Documentary Series. He was the executive producer for the documentary *Man in the Arena*.

He also won the *Sports Illustrated* Sportsman of the Year twice in 2005 and 2021 respectively.

In 2007, he was named Associated Press Male Athlete of the Year.

Tom Brady is also a 5-time ESPY Award winner:

- He won the Best Male Athlete in 2021

- He also won Best NFL Player three times

- In 2021 he won the Outstanding Team Award with his then team Tampa Bay Buccaneers.

Another of Tom Brady's notable honors is appearing on *Time's* 100 Most Influential List.

Tom's NFL Awards:

- He won the Super Bowl MVP 5 times (XXXVI, XXXVIII, XLIX, LI, LV)

- He was also NFC Champion in 2020

- He is a 7 times Super Bowl Champion (XXXVI, XXXVIII, XXXIX, XLIX, LI, LIII, LV)

- He is a 9 times AFC Champion (2001, 2003, 2004, 2007, 2011, 2014, 2016–2018)

- He is a 3 times NFL MVP (2007, 2010, 2017)

- He was part of the 2000s All-Decade Team

- He was part of the 2010s All-Decade Team

- NFL 100th Anniversary All-Time Team

- He won the Bert Bell Award in 2007

- In 2021, he won the FedEx Air NFL Player of The Year Award

- He won NFL Offensive Player of the Year two times in 2007 and 2010, respectively.

- He won NFL Comeback Player of the Year in 2009

- He is a 3-time First-Team All-Pro (2007, 2010, 2017)

- He is also a 3-time Second-Team All-Pro (2005, 2016, 2021)

- 15 times Pro Bowl selection (2001, 2004, 2005, 2007, 2009–2018, 2021)

NCAA

- Tom Brady won the National Champion for Associated Press in 1997.

Tom Brady's Charity and Advocacy Work

Other than his notable football achievements and honors, Tom has worked with a few charity organizations. As this NFL Champion has made quite a fortune from his career and other endorsements, he decided to give back to society. He has currently worked with six charity organizations. One of the charities he works with is known as Best Buddies International. The goal of this charity is to help millions of people with disabilities, whether emotional or physical, fit into the world. It aims toward helping kids with such disabilities make friends in school; for adults, it works to help them get jobs to live normal life. The charity raises its funds through a challenge called the Best Buddies Challenge in which Tom participated. He has been supporting the charity for over 10 years now, and in 2019, he was announced as the global ambassador of the organization. In the course of working and supporting this charity, Tom has been able to gather over $46 million for the benefit of this charity.

Another charity that Tom is known to support is the Entertainment Industry Foundation. This charity foundation deals with creating awareness and also raising funds for various activities either at the local, national, or global level. It is, however, unknown the total amount Tom donated to this foundation.

Tom's support for charity organizations also extends to the Boys and Girls Club of America. This is a program that works towards helping children attain their full potential. To help the program, Tom Brady had his hair shaved at Gillette headquarters. As a result, Gillette donated $35,000 to a Boys and Girls Club in their locality.

What's more, is that Tom showed his care for kids and desire to help them by supporting Kaboom. Kaboom is a charity organization that works towards creating playgrounds for children around the country. Along with other celebrities, United Healthcare and even the Boys and Girls Club, Tom included, they decided to build a playground in the city of Boston, Massachusetts.

His help towards kids doesn't stop here. Just like other celebrities who participated in Make A Wish Foundation, Tom Brady is no exception. He volunteered once in 2017 and took a tour of Gillette Stadium along with nine kids. He and the kids hung out together by watching movies and taking pictures with the trophies won by Tom Brady's team. In 2019, Tom was said to have done something similar again with five children from the Make A Wish Foundation.

Tom participated in a golf tournament organized by Capital One The Match in 2020. This event had to do with some charity functions and so got well-known celebrities to participate in it, after which they donated money to charity organizations like Feeding America and others.

Despite participating in so many charitable events, Tom Brady still took it upon himself to co-found his charity organization known as TB12 Foundation. The main idea behind establishing this organization was to help other athletes like Tom. The foundation was established in 2015, and it aims to ensure athletes have the necessary medical care, nutritional benefits, and cognitive support they'll require to perform well and succeed. It has been recorded from a legitimate source that the foundation organizes an annual marathon in Boston to raise money for its cause. In 2019, the marathon held was said to raise an estimate of $125,000.

"Máximas da noite... 'você tem na 26 anos?' TSC (Claro, que não) e 'você é parente do Tom Brady? o marido da Gisele' (Claro, ele não sabe disso #primo)" by noxCowboy is licensed under CC BY 2.0.

Tom Brady's Timeline

1977 - Thomas Brady was born on the 3rd of August in San Mateo, California.

1995 - He was drafted by the Montreal Expos in the MLB Draft. Tom also entered the University of Michigan and joined the Michigan Wolverines football team.

1996 - Tom Brady played his first college game on September 26, 1996.

1997 - Tom won the National Champion for Associated Press.

April 2000 - During the sixth round, Tom finally was picked by coach Bill Belichick of the New England Patriots. He also began the season as the fourth-string quarterback.

September 2001 - During the 2001 season, Tom Brady replaced Drew Bledsoe as the starting quarterback for the Patriots. He also led the team in the game against the Indianapolis Colts. The Patriots won the game 44-13.

January 2002 - Tom Brady won his first playoff game.

February 2002 - Tom Brady won his first Super Bowl. He also won MVP at the Super Bowl. He was the youngest Super Bowl-winning quarterback.

2002 - Tom's team sadly didn't make it to the playoffs. The Patriots also didn't win at least 10 games.

2003 - Tom had an injured shoulder before the season started. However, Tom's team had fifteen wins in a row, unlike the previous season.

February 2004 - Tom Brady won his second Super Bowl.

February 2005 - Tom Brady won his third Super Bowl. It was his first back-to-back Super Bowl win.

2005 - Tom won the *Sports Illustrated* Sportsman of the year award. The Patriots also made it to the playoffs.

December 2007 - Tom set the record for the NFL single-season touchdown.

January 2008 - The only Patriots were involved in the Spygate scandal.

February 2008 - Tom Brady was awarded his first NFL MVP. Tom also got his first Super Bowl loss.

September 2008 - Tom was injured during the season opener and was replaced by Matt Cassel for the rest of the season.

2009 - Tom married Gisele Bündchen and welcomed his second son, Benjamin Rein.

February 2010 - Tom won the NFL Comeback Player of the Year.

February 2011 - Tom won NFL Offensive Player of the Year and also his second NFL MVP award.

September 2011 - Tom Brady hits Wes Welker for a 99-yard touchdown. It was the 12th that was ever thrown at this time.

February 2012 - Tom Brady lost his second Super Bowl.

2012 - Tom welcomed his third child, Vivian Lake Brady.

January 2015 - Tom Brady was involved in the deflategate scandal. They said he used deflated footballs.

February 2015 - Tom Brady won his fourth Super Bowl. He was also awarded his third NFL MVP.

May 2015 - Tom Brady was suspended for four games in the coming season.

September 2015 - The second circuit court of appeal made a rolling nullifying Tom Brady's suspension.

2015 - He also broke the record of postseason touchdowns and also has the most yardage in a career. Tom also co-founded the TB12 Foundation for charity purposes.

2017 - Tom Brady made the best Super Bowl comeback of all time.

February 2018 - He won his third MVP award. He became the oldest player to receive the award. He got his fifth Super Bowl loss.

February 2019 - Tom Brady won his sixth Super Bowl. He became the oldest quarterback to less his team to the Superbowl.

2019 - His foundation, TB12, organized a marathon and raised $125,000.

March 2020 - Tom Brady announced that he was leaving the New England Patriots and joining the Tampa Bay Buccaneers.

February 2021 - Tom Brady won his seventh Super Bowl.

2021 - Tom won the FedEx Air NFL Player of the Year Award. He also won the *Sports Illustrated* Sportsman of the year award. The last time he won the award was back in 2005.

References

General

Tom Brady: An Unauthorized Biography by Belmont and Belcourt Biographies. Scribd.

https://www.scribd.com/book/153492995

Introduction

https://www.insider.com/tom-brady-fun-facts-new-england-patriots-tampa-bay-buccaneers-2022-2?amp

College Career

https://vault.si.com/.amp/vault/2012/01/09/tom-brady-as-you-forgot-him

https://www.si.com/college/ohiostate/.amp/football/ohio-state-football-looking-back-tom-brady-career-against-buckeyes-michigan-wolverines-nfl-retirement

Rookie Years

https://www.si.com/.amp/nfl/2021/08/30/tales-of-tom-brady-forgotten-rookie-year-2000-season-daily-cover

2002 Season

https://www.pro-football-reference.com/teams/nwe/2002.htm

2003 Season

https://www.pro-football-reference.com/teams/nwe/2003.htm

2004 Season

https://www.pro-football-reference.com/teams/nwe/2004.htm

2005 Season

https://www.pro-football-reference.com/teams/nwe/2005.htm

2006 Season

https://www.pro-football-reference.com/teams/nwe/2006.htm

2007 Season

https://www.espn.com/nfl/story/_/id/20284825/the-tom-brady-bill-belichick-shift-how-2007-new-england-patriots-super-bowl-spygate-changed-everything

https://www.pro-football-reference.com/teams/nwe/2007.htm

2008 Season

https://www.pro-football-reference.com/teams/nwe/2008.htm

2009 Season

https://www.pro-football-reference.com/teams/nwe/2009.htm

2010 Season

https://www.pro-football-reference.com/teams/nwe/2010.htm

https://www.statmuse.com/nfl/ask/tom-brady-2010-season

2011 Season

https://www.pro-football-reference.com/teams/nwe/2011.htm

https://www.espn.com/nfl/recap/_/gameId/311030023?platform=amp

2012 Season

https://www.pro-football-reference.com/teams/nwe/2012.htm

2013 Season

https://www.pro-football-reference.com/teams/nwe/2013.htm

2014 Season

https://www.pro-football-reference.com/teams/nwe/2014.htm

2015 Season

https://www.pro-football-reference.com/teams/nwe/2015.htm

2016 Season

https://www.pro-football-reference.com/teams/nwe/2016.htm

2017 Season

https://www.pro-football-reference.com/teams/nwe/2017.htm

2018 Season

https://www.pro-football-reference.com/teams/nwe/2018.htm

2019 Season

https://www.pro-football-reference.com/teams/nwe/2019.htm

2020 Season

https://www.pro-football-reference.com/teams/tam/2020.htm

https://www.usatoday.com/story/sports/nfl/2021/07/15/tom-brady-played-entire-2020-season-with-torn-mcl/117533872/

2021 Season

https://www.si.com/.amp/nfl/2022/06/02/tom-brady-explains-why-he-came-out-of-retirement-after-one-month

Timeline

https://www.abcactionnews.com/sports/football/tampa-bay-bucs/timeline-a-look-back-at-tom-bradys-historic-career?_amp=true

https://www.tampabay.com/sports/bucs/2020/03/17/timeline-the-highs-and-lows-of-tom-bradys-nfl-career/?outputType=amp

Final Surprise Bonus

Hope you've enjoyed this biography of Tom Brady.

We always like to give more than we get, so I'd like to give you one final bonus.

Do me a favor, if you enjoyed this book, *please* leave a review on Amazon.

It'll help get the word out so more kids can find out more about Tom Brady!

If you do, I'll send you one of my most cherished video collection – Free:

Ultimate Collection of Links to Tom Brady's YouTube Videos!

You won't be able to say you know Tom Brady until you watch these videos!

Here's how to claim your free videos:

1. Leave a review right away -

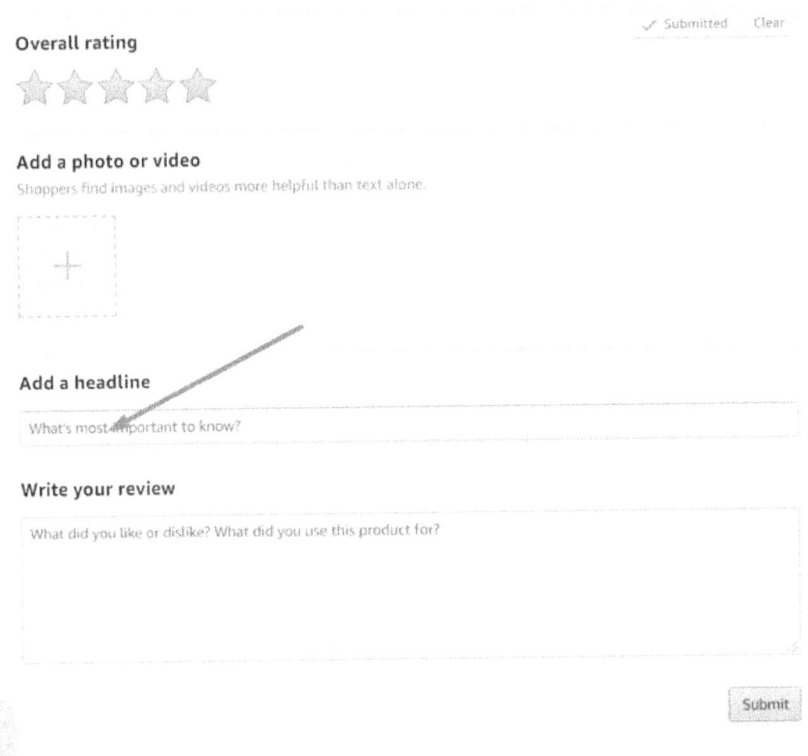

Overall rating

✓ Submitted   Clear

Add a photo or video
Shoppers find images and videos more helpful than text alone.

Add a headline

What's most important to know?

Write your review

What did you like or dislike? What did you use this product for?

Submit

2. Send a screenshot of your review to: reviews@allaboutbookseries.com with the subject line: All About Tom Brady Review

3. Receive your free video collection – "Ultimate Collection of Links to Tom Brady's YouTube Videos! " – *immediately*!